MEMPHIS STATE UNIVERSITY
3 2109 00480 9712

D1032343

Financial Policies In Transition:

A Critique Of Selected Issues, 1967

THE M. L. SEIDMAN MEMORIAL
TOWN HALL LECTURE SERIES

MEMPHIS STATE UNIVERSITY

The M. L. Seidman Memorial Town Hall Lecture Series was established by P. K. Seidman in memory of his late brother, M. L. Seidman, founder of the firm Seidman and Seidman, Certified Public Accountants.

Publication of this book was made possible by a gift from Mr. P. K. Seidman to the Memphis State University Press.

Financial Policies In Transition:

A Critique Of Selected Issues, 1967

edited by Thomas O. Depperschmidt
Professor of Economics
Memphis State University

MEMPHIS STATE UNIVERSITY PRESS
MEMPHIS, TENNESSEE 1968

PRINTED BY CREATIVE PRINTING DIVISION,
INTERNATIONAL GRAPHICS INC.
LITTLE ROCK, ARKANSAS

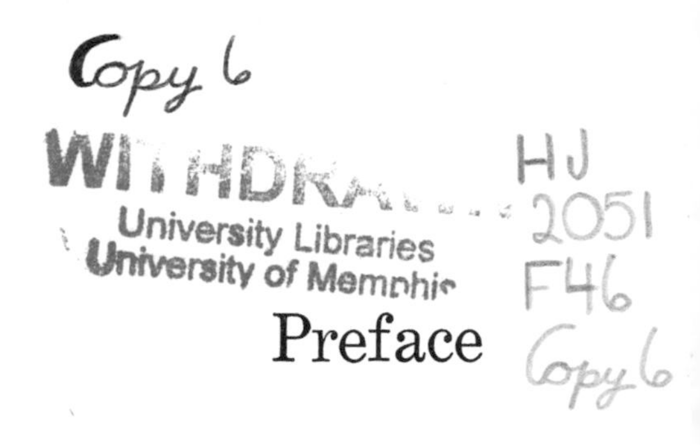

Preface

As envisioned by its founder, the M. L. Seidman Memorial Town Hall Lecture Series is to provide community programs of excellence in public affairs. P. K. Seidman therein is creating a fitting, continuing memorial to his late brother and business partner, M. L. Seidman, in the firm Seidman and Seidman, Certified Public Accountants.

M. L. Seidman's interest in public finance spanned several decades. He served as a consultant to congressional tax committees, as a syndicated columnist, and as an appointed delegate (by three New York governors) to conventions of the National Tax Association. He served for a time on the executive committee of the New York Board of Trade. In addition, he was active in professional organizations in his field, such as the American Institute of Certified Public Accountants and the New York State Society of Certified Public Accountants. His firm, based in New York, continues in his tradition an enviable reputation of professional and community service.

To implement the educational and community service concepts of the Lecture Series, its coordinating committee developed a format to engage creators and administrators of public policy in lecture programs. The guiding principle was the direct transmission of policy design and detail procedures to an audience by public figures. In 1967, the first year of the Lecture Series, the speaker-participants invited to the Memphis State University campus appeared at dinner conferences with faculty, formal colloquies with faculty and students, formal and informal discussion groups following the lectures, and at the formal lectures. In many respects, the speakers' secondary appearances were most indicative of their personality and political talents.

Indeed, the conceptual strength of the Series was rivaled only by the brilliance and renown of the guest lecturers in its initial year. In the order of their appearance in the Series, the contributors were: Dr. Raymond J. Saulnier, Professor of Economics at Columbia University, author, consultant and officer in numerous government and research agencies and for four years chairman of former President Eisenhower's Council of Economic Advisers; James J. Saxon, at the time of the lecture co-chairman of the Board of the American Fletcher National Bank of Indianapolis, for many years an official with the U. S. Treasury Department, an American delegate to several major international monetary conferences, and Comptroller of the Currency, 1961-1966; Pierre-Paul Schweitzer, former director of the French Treasury and Deputy Governor of the Bank of France, since 1963 Managing Director and Chairman of the Board of the International Monetary Fund. In its goal of providing public contact with distinguished lecturers, grounded in academic tradition and broadened in the crucible of public service experience, the coordinating committee of the Seidman Lecture Series realized its ideal of excellence.

* * *

In his presentation, "Three Federal Budget Concepts: Which is 'Best'?", Dr. Saulnier is concerned with the calculation of the budget rather than the deficit or surplus condition that might exist. He deplores the absence of the

Johnson Administration's explanation for the apparent demise of the unofficial "high employment budget" concept, since it was at one time a highly touted budgetary guideline and was used as the basis of criticism of the Saulnier period with the Council of Economic Advisers. Professor Saulnier's discussion of the three-budget concepts still in use centers on the extent of coverage and the matter of timing in calculating each of the budgets. These differences he notes to be substantial.

The mechanics of calculating each budget, while mutually inconsistent among the three, nonetheless must provide a basis for judgement and action by various arms of government. Because the responsibility of Congress differs for "federal funds" and "trust funds," both the administrative budget and some form of trust fund accounting are indispensable to its financial deliberations. The Treasury, on the other hand, having two major operating responsibilities in the public debt and cash balance of the federal government, finds both the administrative and cash budgets critically important; the "federal sector of the national income accounts" is only of passing interest. The latter is also of little use to monetary authorities concerned with the fiscal impact on the capital markets. The cash consolidated statement is better, but it is also limited because this accounting of loan ("participation certificate") sales by government has the effect of minimizing government spending and the deficit. Monetary authorities find the "cash budget adjusted for financial asset sales," not one of the three standard, unrefined budgets, the best measure of the effect of federal fiscal operations on the capital markets. To the economic forecaster, the federal sector of the national income accounts is a standard source of data. But it too is deficient in registering the impact on the capital markets of federal fiscal activity.

Because each budget is useful only to certain groups and is deficient in other circumstances, Professor Saulnier concludes that no one budget account is "best." He recommends continued presentation of all three, with important qualifications to increase the usefulness of the cash consolidated statement. He urges the structuring of a bipartisan committee to review budgetary procedure with the object of improving account presentation, thereby increasing the value of such data to the major users.

Mr. Saxon's treatise, "Public Regulation of Private Financial Resources," first reviews financial problems surrounding the evolution of the three principal bank regulating agencies, notes some current trends in the competitive environment of banking, and closes with a careful evaluation of the controversy over mergers and competition in banking.

An interesting aspect of the historical review of regulatory agencies is Mr. Saxon's recounting of the sometimes strained relations between Federal Reserve authorities and the Comptroller's office over bank supervision by the respective agencies. Mr. Saxon views the advent of the FDIC in the 1930s primarily from the viewpoint of bank supervision, the area where the FDIC's authority most nearly competes with that of the Comptroller and the Federal Reserve banks. Particularly significant is his comment that bank reform legislation, typically passed in a crisis situation, quickly becomes anachronistic when the crisis fades. Not only has duplication and overlap of authority ensued from this legislative indirection, but the institutional rigidities created thereby have thwarted regulatory flexibility, making bank supervision most difficult.

By contrast, Mr. Saxon says, banks themselves, threatened with nonbank intermediaries' competition, have now come out of the overly conservative mentality of the 1920s through the 1940s. He cites the changed bank account ratios reflecting this competitive trend. Changes in Regulation Q governing time deposits, reintroduction of the negotiable certificate of deposit, and the issue of debt obligations by banks further evidence and abet the competitive revival of banks.

In the third section of his paper, Mr. Saxon visits again the scene of controversy surrounding major decisions of his tenure as Comptroller. His commitment to competition in banking is straightforward and generally supported outside the banking community. And his policy decision to encourage chartering of new banks and creation of branches is consistent with that commitment. However, a major indicator of the controversy over bank mergers, supported selectively by the Comptroller's Office, is court reluctance to except banks from anti-trust prosecution. Not surprisingly, Mr. Saxon would favor definitive, statutory clarification of banks' liability under anti-trust laws and of the supervisory domain of the three regulatory agencies.

Mr. Schweitzer in "The International Monetary System and the Fund," answers criticism of the Fund and its operation without identifying sources. He denies that current criticism is more intense than in earlier years of its relatively short history.

Mr. Schweitzer seeks first, through an historical examination of "The Gold Problem," to explain the likely reasons for some of the confusion in public media and among laymen about international finances. He notes as a distinctive feature of current debate the fact that "the accepted area of economic policy has widened." Modern governments accept responsibility for total domestic economic performance, including employment and growth. Their concern is no longer limited to exchange stability. And service of competing domestic goals complicates international financial policy while it constrains domestic policy. Indeed, the scheme of the International Monetary Fund, Mr. Schweitzer says, is to permit governments to resolve domestic economic problems without being forced to adopt defensive and restrictive international policies. Thus, in describing the par value system, he remarks that the responsibility of managing economies caused governments to insist that exchange rates not be entirely outside their control; yet this control could not be exercised through each government's independent action since currencies other than those of the initiating government would be affected.

Has the Fund performed this function of regulating member countries' financial and trade affairs with each other? In answering "yes," Mr. Schweitzer points to the absence of competitive currency devaluation, the steady freeing of international transactions from trade and payments restrictions, and the increasing reliance of members on the Fund, reflected in summary statistics of the Fund's operations during its first two decades. Furthermore, Fund operations reinforce international confidence. The reputation established by a country's qualifying for Fund assistance may dissolve the hesitation of other lenders to that country.

Mr. Schweitzer notes an "increasingly important byproduct" of Fund activities in recent years: the creation of international reserves. Moreover, drawings on the Fund, almost exclusively in the form of United States dollars prior to 1961, have since broadened to include other currencies (18 in all), some of these of developing countries. Overall Fund reserves and world reserves have increased markedly since the late 1950s. Mr. Schweitzer concludes, however, that "assessment of the appropriate level of world reserves and of the appropriate rate of reserve growth is still an indescribably difficult task." He approves the "universal agreement" that the reserve base of the system should be brought under deliberate control. He sees the agreement and discussions underlying it as much needed clarification of issues and a major step toward resolving the continuing problems of international finance.

* * *

Memphis State University, the sponsor and site of the M. L. Seidman Memorial Lecture Series, in many respects is the direct beneficiary of the Series. The design of the Series is not to appeal solely to an academic audience, however. The availability of these lectures when presented to the people of Memphis and its metropolitan area, and now to the community at large in this permanent form, attests to the abiding concern of the Series founder and its coordinating committee for education in public affairs.

For the committee*
Dr. Thomas O. Depperschmidt
Professor of Economics
Memphis State University

*Frank R. Ahlgren, Editor
The (Memphis) *Commercial Appeal*

Dr. Ronald E. Carrier, Provost
Memphis State University

Dr. Herbert J. Markle, Dean
The College of Business Administration
Memphis State University

Lewis K. McKee, President
National Bank of Commerce

P. K. Seidman, Partner
Seidman and Seidman, CPA

Dr. Festus J. Viser, Chairman
Department of Economics
Memphis State University

Financial Policies In Transition:
A Critique Of Selected Issues, 1967

"Three Federal Budget Concepts: Which is 'Best'?"

Lecture One

by Dr. Raymond J. Saulnier

My subject is the federal budget, not whether it makes any difference how the budget comes out in the end (whether there is a deficit or a surplus) but how the deficit or the surplus, as the case may be, is calculated. To put it differently, my subject is federal budget accounting.

Such a subject would in any case be appropriate for a lecture memorializing a distinguished public accountant, but for a number of reasons it is also a topical one. First, a budget that is deeply and consistently in deficit on any recognized and respected method of accounting is bound to become a conversation piece. And the federal budget is deeply in deficit and has been for six full fiscal years. It is now in its seventh deficit year, and there are additional deficits ahead, even under the most optimistic assumptions concerning economic developments. And because we have been running large deficits during prosperity, the deficits that would emerge if the economy were to turn into recession would be enormous.

Second, it is a good rule that when some aspect of the economy gets out of kilter, so to speak, debate tends to center on the statistics that bear on the problem. That rule has not failed in the present case. What has attracted particular attention is that there are three different sets of figures on the budget and that each tells a different story. On one basis of calculation we have had deficits of only $4.8 billion in the past six full fiscal years; on a second basis, we have had nearly $23 billion; and on a third, we have in this period had a deficiency of receipts below expenditures of just over $30 billion.

Third, it did not go unnoticed that the administration's recent choice of the budget concept which, in its opinion, is the best measure of the federal government's economic impact happens to be the concept that shows the smallest deficit.

Finally, the subject is topical also because the President has indicated he will appoint a bipartisan group to study federal budget accounting practices and make recommendations for improved methods of presenting the figures.

I shall (1) attempt to explain the several budget concepts (2) discuss their relative merits for measuring the federal government's impact on the economy and (3) make suggestions for presenting federal budget accounts.

The Several Budget Concepts

There are three budget concepts that warrant particular attention. I will mention a fourth, one that seems recently to have been lost in the shuffle, but there are only three that figure in the current dialogue. These are: (1) the administrative budget (the budget most familiar in public discussion) (2) the cash consolidated statement (better known as the cash budget) and (3) the so-called NIA budget. Since the last is not a budget at all, I will not refer to it as such, but rather by its technical name: the "federal sector of the national income and product accounts."

The fourth budget concept, to which I just alluded, must be referred to in the past tense, since it has apparently been abandoned for official use. I refer to the "full employment surplus concept," or what came to be known as the "high-employment budget." It was prominently set forth in the January, 1962, *Economic Report* and in the 1965 *Report* was praised as "a useful measure of the impact of the federal budget on economic activity." There was not a word about it, however, in the last two *Economic Reports.* On the contrary, the administration has now turned to the federal sector of the national income and product accounts as its preferred method of measuring federal government impact on the economy.

I have no wish to comment more than parenthetically on the mysterious disappearance of the "full employment surplus concept." But I am constrained to say that if it was dropped because it is giving wrong signals now as to what fiscal policy ought to be, or gave wrong signals in the past, then the public deserves an explanation of what is officially thought to be wrong with this previously much-admired concept. It never seemed to me to be a good one, and I have publicly presented my objections to it; but it was, after all, the intellectual foundation of fiscal policy in recent years. Moreover, and this is a point on which I concede a certain personal interest, it was used extensively by officers of government since 1960 to disparage the fiscal policies of the nineteen-fifties. Remembering this, some explanation is called for if the concept is now being cast aside as somehow seriously deficient. At least, it deserves an obituary notice.

How the Several Budget Concepts Differ

Let me turn now to a description of the three federal budget concepts still in circulation and competing for attention. How do they differ, one from another?

There are a good many differences, but they fall mainly into two general groups. The first has to do with coverage, that is, with the extent to which the concepts include federal fiscal transactions within their scope. The second has to do with the basis on which the several concepts register the occurrence of transactions, which we may refer to as the criterion of timing.

In Coverage

On the coverage question, let me note at once that no one of the concepts covers all federal fiscal transactions. In each case there is a certain amount of offsetting of receipts against expenditures with the result that substantial areas of government spending are never visible in the budget. Business-type activities of the federal government, such as the Post Office and TVA, are reported this way. And, as we will see later, federal lending operations are reported on a net basis. However, except for the handling of lending programs, we can ignore for present purposes those limitations of coverage in respect of which the several budget concepts are the same; all that concerns us here are the ways in which the coverage of the three budget concepts is significantly different.

Briefly, the important differences of coverage are that the administrative budget excludes trust fund operations, whereas the cash budget and the federal sector of the national income accounts include them, and that both the administrative budget and the cash budget cover transactions of federal lending programs, whereas the federal sector of the national income accounts does not. Thus, the most complete set of accounts is the cash budget; it includes trust fund operations absent in the administrative budget and lending transactions absent in the national income accounts. If there is merit in breadth of coverage —and I believe there is—the blue ribbon, on this score, goes to the cash budget.

In Timing

Let us now look at the three concepts from the point of view of their timing of transactions. Conceptually, two bases are used: transactions are recorded on a *current* basis, that is, as they actually occur, or on an *accrual* basis, that is, as rights to receive income, or liability to pay taxes or make other payments are incurred.

It would be convenient if we could say that the three budget concepts are consistent, each within itself, in following either a current or an accrual form of accounting but this is apparently not strictly the case. Broadly speaking, however, we may note that the cash and the administrative budgets are on a current basis and that the federal sector of the national income accounts is on an accrual basis. Thus, the administrative and cash budgets register spending as it occurs—with the interesting but not very significant difference that the former registers spending as checks are drawn while the latter registers it as checks pass through clearance—whereas the national income accounts record spending for equipment and supplies at time of delivery, regardless of when money to pay for them is actually disbursed. On the income side, the administrative and cash budgets record revenues as they are actually received, though again with the minor difference between writing and clearing checks, whereas the national income accounts register receipts from corporate income taxes not as companies actually pay them but as their liability to pay taxes accrues.

So much for the major differences among the three concepts. What I have noted, plus other points of lesser importance, are set forth clearly in the January 1967 budget document.

Uses And Relative Merits Of Budget Concepts

What are we to conclude as to the relative merits of these three budget concepts for measuring the impact of federal fiscal transactions on the economy?

The administration has recently stated that it is the federal sector of the national income accounts that is "best" in this connection, but "best" in this context must be a relative matter. There is no absolute best. A particular budget concept can be "best" only in the sense that in a particular use it serves better than any other. If there were only one use to which budget concepts are put, we could expect a definitive answer to the question: which concept is best? But there is a variety of uses and no *a priori* reason to say that any one concept is "best" in connection with all of them.

For the Congress

Consider first the use to which Congress puts the various budgets. Obviously, Congress must be interested in all three concepts, but it has a particular interest in the administrative budget. It is this set of accounts—and no other set—that deals specifically and exclusively with fiscal transactions for which Congress has a unique operating responsibility. If one examines the appendix to the budget document, he will find that transactions are organized into two categories, those involving "federal funds" and those involving "trust funds." Federal funds are those which, as the budget document puts it, "are owned by the federal government." Their hallmark is that they are funds in respect of which Congress stands in a kind of proprietary position, a position that involves both discretionary authority and special responsibility.

With respect to "trust funds" on the other hand, Congress stands in a position of trustee or fiduciary. These include social security and unemployment insurance trust funds, the highway trust fund, funds of several federally-sponsored enterprises, of which FDIC is an example, and funds left with the federal government in a kind of "suspense" category or as a deposit. Responsibility of the Congress for trust funds is essentially different from responsibility of the Congress for federally-owned funds; accordingly, separate accounting of the two is necessary.

For the Congress, the administrative budget—which records transactions in federal funds—is not only a meaningful but an indispensable set of accounts. It has been correctly described in the budget document as "the focal point for management and decision-making with respect to government activities financed by the government's own funds." Ultimately to consolidate administrative budget and trust fund transactions in a single accounting statement (as in the cash consolidated statement) does not in any way interfere with the carrying out by Congress of its responsibilities for the two separate types of funds. Indeed, the cash consolidated statement provides Congress with much valuable information. The point is that, with the responsibilities of Congress defined as they are, it needs an administrative budget and it needs separate trust fund accounts. The much maligned administrative budget has obvious deficiencies for measuring the impact of federal fiscal transactions on the economy; all the same, it is an indispensable accounting concept for the Congress.

For the Treasury

The Treasury has two major operating responsibilities that determine what it needs by way of budget accounts. These are its responsibilities for the public debt and for the cash balance of the federal government. Changes in the amount of public debt outstanding are affected by changes in government cash balances and by financing transactions of government enterprises, but they are determined primarily by transactions in federally-owned funds, as reflected in the administrative budget. Changes in the government's public financing requirements, on the other hand, are affected not only by transactions in federally-owned funds but by transactions in trust funds as well. Accordingly, from a purely functional point of view, the administrative budget is indispensable to the Treasury for its management of cash and total public debt, and the cash budget is indispensable to it for the conduct of public debt-financing operations. If the Treasury had no administrative budget or no cash budget, it would have to invent both all over again, and would have to do so promptly.

The federal sector of the national income accounts is another matter. The Secretary of the Treasury uses these data in certain broad analyses, but if they were all he had to guide him in the performance of his duties as chief financial officer of the federal government he could be swamped with cash; more serious, he could see his checks returned marked "no funds" and not have the slightest forewarning of these embarrassments. Nor would he have the least idea of the kind of debt-financing problem he was up against. In short, for the Treasury, the national income accounts are interesting but the administrative budget and the cash budget are indispensable.

For the Monetary Authorities and Financial Analysts

Consider next the needs of those who must evaluate the impact of federal fiscal transactions on the capital markets. These are questions of paramount interest to the nation's monetary authorities—the Treasury and the Federal Reserve System—and to scores of businessmen and financial analysts.

The point is that the federal sector of the national income accounts is of little direct use in making financial analyses. Because they exclude government lending operations they give an incomplete measure of the amount of funds the federal government is injecting into the economy, and an incomplete measure of what government is demanding from the capital markets. For such measures, one has to turn to the cash consolidated statement. And even this statement, with its extensive coverage of financial transactions, is still not broad enough to measure the federal government's full financial impact on the economy. This deficiency results from the way the cash consolidated statement handles the sale of financial assets by the federal government.

For example: because it is a banker nowadays on a very large scale—far larger than is commonly understood—the federal government holds large amounts of financial assets. In fiscal 1966, it entered into new direct loan commitments amounting to $7.2 billion, entirely apart from the $24.3 billion of privately advanced loans which it committed itself to insure or guarantee, and its holdings of loans amounted to $33 billion at the end of that fiscal period. Recently, however, it has been selling loans from among these holdings, not in small amounts, as was done in the 1950s, but in very large amounts. Thus, in fiscal 1966 it sold nearly $3 billion; it proposes to sell another $4 billion in fiscal 1967; and budget plans for fiscal 1968 call for sales of $5.3 billion.

In the 1950s, loans were sold in order to get the federal government out of the banking business, but that is obviously not the purpose of recent sales since (except to a minor extent) loans are not turned over to the buyer but are held in a special trust fund and continue to be serviced by the federal government. What is sold is a security called a "participation certificate" or PC, which has been ruled by the Attorney General to be backed by the "full faith and credit of the United States."

The effect of these sales on the budget is to make spending and the deficit seem less than they really are. Because the sale of financial assets is treated as a loan repayment, and because loan repayments are netted against loan disbursements in reporting expenditures, net budget expenditures for lending agencies and, therefore, net expenditures for the administrative and cash budgets are less, dollar for dollar, than they would otherwise be. And because recorded expenditures are less, the recorded deficit is less. Thus, as a result of financial asset sales, the federal government appears to be spending less than it is actually spending and its budget deficit appears to be less than it actually is. The federal sector of the national income accounts is, of course, entirely innocent of this effect because it excludes lending transactions altogether.

Because PC sales are as much a security flotation as

the issuance of conventional federal debt, if we want to measure capital requirements of the federal government we have to add their sales to the deficit recorded in the cash budget. Similarly, to get a meaningful measure of the change in federal debt, we must add outstanding participation certificates to the amount of outstanding conventional debt.

The budget concept that best measures the extent to which federal fiscal operations affect capital markets is neither the administrative budget nor the cash budget, and certainly not the federal sector of the national income accounts; it is the cash budget adjusted for financial asset sales.

For Policymakers and Economists

Finally, we come to the task of evaluating the impact of federal fiscal operations on the economy as a whole. It is this task—wider than the task of evaluating the impact on credit markets—that is faced by the economic forecaster; it is a major preoccupation, also, of federal policymakers.

Because what happens to capital markets is a major consideration in determining what will happen to the economy, and because it is the cash budget adjusted for financial asset sales that reveals this impact, we may begin by saying that a critical part of the task of evaluating the federal government's impact on the economy as a whole must be satisfied by the cash budget adjusted for financial asset sales. Not only does this measure government financing requirements, but it gives some clue as to whether their satisfaction will involve recourse to the commercial banking system, and thus whether it will affect the money supply. We may differ in the importance we attach to changes in the money supply, but there can be no quarrel with the proposition that, if we don't know how government operations are affecting the money supply, we are without a major part of an explanation of how it is affecting the economy generally. And I emphasize again that, in supplying information to this end, the federal sector of the national income accounts gives no help at all. What information we have comes from the cash budget adjusted for financial asset sales.

Last summer was an object lesson in what we need to know if we are to understand how the federal government affects the economy. A near-crisis was brought on by a sudden turn to tightness in monetary policy concurrently with massive and untimely sales of participation certificates. As a register of these near-calamitous events, the federal sector of the national income accounts is a complete blank! It is a remarkable thing that in a world where there is so much preoccupation with interest rates and with tight money and easy money, the budget concept officially labeled as "best" in revealing the impact of federal operations on the economy should tell us nothing *directly* about the forces affecting interest rates, credit markets, or the money supply. Trying to understand the impact of federal fiscal operations on the economy solely by the use of national income accounts is like trying to understand the impact of consumer spending on the economy without knowing what is happening to consumer credit. It is impossible.

What the national income accounts do for us, and it is an undeniably useful service, is to measure the direct impact of federal operations in national income and production. Important as this is, however, it does not justify labeling that set of accounts "best" for measuring the government's impact on the economy. This much is clear: if all we knew about the impact of the federal government on the economy was what we could learn from the federal sector of the national income accounts, we would promptly have to reinvent the cash budget. And when we had reinvented the cash budget we would have to learn how to adjust it for sales of financial assets.

THE MERITS OF ACCRUAL VERSUS CURRENT ACCOUNTING

Let me touch briefly on another point frequently mentioned as a particular merit of the national accounts, namely, that they measure federal financial transactions on an accrual rather than on a current basis. There is a good deal to be said for accrual accounting in evaluating the impact of the federal government on the economy; but it is debatable whether, from an economic point of view, it is the "best" basis of accounting. For example, consider the handling of government revenues. Do taxes have more impact on a corporate taxpayer when he makes the cash payment or when he accrues his tax liability? The use of cash to pay taxes affects corporate liquidity; the accrual of taxes does not. Accrued tax liabilities, on the other hand, affect corporate income and profits, whereas disbursement of cash to pay taxes does not. Which is more important, the impact on liquidity or the impact on income? No analyst can afford to be interested in one to the exclusion of the other. To say that the national income accounts are "best" because they are put together on an accrual basis is not at all a conclusive argument.

On the same point, consider the merits of accrual *versus* current accounting in recording federal expenditures. Is it more useful to know when federal spending actually takes place, that is, when checks are drawn or cashed, or to know when the goods for which these payments are made are delivered? My answer to that question is that the analyst must be interested in knowing both when the payments are made and when the goods are delivered. One should be eclectic in these things; one needs all the information available. Information on the flow of cash comes from the cash budget; information on the flow of goods comes from the national products accounts. Nothing could be more fruitless than an attempt to show that one type of information is more important or somehow better than the other.

Up-To-Dateness

This discussion can be concluded by pointing out that of the three budget concepts the federal sector of the national income accounts must get the lowest rating when judged by the time-lag between the information it supplies and actual events. The administrative budget is available on a monthly basis. The same is true of the cash budget. The national income accounts are available only quarterly, and even at that, with a considerable time-lag. Thus, if you were to look now (March, 1967) for the most up-to-date information available in the federal sector of the national income accounts you would find some information through December 1966; but for the budget deficit or surplus you would find data only through September of last year. We may sometime have monthly data on national income and product accounts, and the sooner the better, but as things stand these estimates have the weakness of lagging very much behind events.

Conclusions And Recommendations

(1) President Johnson's plan to appoint a bipartisan com-

mission to review methods of presenting federal budget information and make suggestions for improvement comes at a time when such a review is greatly needed. What the commission should strive for in federal budget accounting is precisely what we insist on in corporate financial accounting: full disclosure; methods of presentation that avoid misunderstanding; accounts that adequately serve the needs of the principal users of budget materials.

(2) There being no one way of presenting federal fiscal information that meets the needs of all users equally well, and as fully as we should strive to meet them, we should continue the present method, which is to present all three accounts. However, when we speak about "budget deficit" or "budget surplus" we should speak of what is shown in the cash consolidated statement. Gaps in coverage seriously impair the usefulness of the administrative budget for such purposes, though it is an indispensable tool in the management of funds for which Congress has special responsibility. The federal sector of the national income and product accounts, though useful in showing the relation between federal activities and changes in national income and production, is open to the same objection. It will help public discourse if the latter is referred to as an "analysis" rather than as a "budget."

(3) Even the cash consolidated statement is inadequate in one of the leading uses to which federal fiscal information is put: to measure the amount of the federal government's current and prospective demands on the capital markets. To correct this inadequacy, the budget document should include a special analysis of the capital market requirements of the federal govern-

ment and related agencies. It would set forth actual results and projections for:

a) change in public debt arising from transactions in federally-owned funds, changes in cash balances and financing transactions by government enterprises.

b) the extent to which federal debt financing is accomplished through absorption of securities by federal trust funds.

c) the extent to which federal expenditures are financed by seigniorage and sales of financial assets, in particular sales of participation certificates.

d) financing by federal agencies that is additive to direct federal financing.

(4) It would be enormously helpful, also, if the federal government were to institute the practice of making quarterly projections of federal expenditures, federal budget receipts and the federal government's capital market requirements. As things stand, information on such matters is more extensive and reliable for the private economy than for the federal government.

(5) In the interest of full disclosure and public understanding, the budget document, through appropriate footnotes or memorandum accounts, should clarify and give prominence to unusual transactions and circumstances affecting the budget. This would include large sales of financial assets, especially participation certificates; unusual gains from seigniorage; and nonrecurring gains or losses of revenue, such as result from changes in methods of tax collection or the management of funds and lending programs. The rule should be the same as that applied to corporate financial accounting: a realistic presentation of budget

results that will make it possible to draw meaningful comparisons between operations in adjoining fiscal years and over longer periods of time.

* * *

It must be conceded that we have been operating of late in a kind of fiscal fog. This is not only unbecoming but downright dangerous. I hope the suggestions made in these remarks will help lift that fog and extend the range of financial and economic visibility.

Lecture Two

by James J. Saxon

It is a special privilege to participate in this distinguished lecture series. The great problems of finance to which your speakers are addressing themselves are among the most important confronting public officials both at home and abroad; their solution through sound and constructive applications of contemporary financial analysis would relieve many of the tensions of the world. In particular, the continuing reluctance of the United States to exercise its present power to remove the harrassing effects of gold as international money has exacerbated domestic stabilization problems and produced a growing estrangement with friends abroad, particularly in western Europe. At home, a persistent refusal to let competitive forces produce financial institutions of optimum size has retarded economic development, particularly in those areas where state laws have been especially restrictive. To these and other questions of public financial policy men of good will must direct continuing attention.

I must confess to a certain apprehension that my remarks will not seem novel. A good deal of what I have to say is now lodged in the public record, though often effectively hidden in the forbidding prose and the jumble of exhibits that are the distinguishing marks of government documents. On the other hand, now some months out of public office I can review dispassionately my years of service as Comptroller of the Currency, assessing as a private citizen the consequences of major steps taken during my tenure.

I shall begin with a reminder of the historical circumstances in which the three federal regulatory agencies assumed their supervisory duties. I will next indicate some currents of recent change in commercial banking, suggesting how change has affected the competitive environment and so the problem of resource allocation in American finance. I will conclude with a prognosis of the near-term outcome of recent controversy that has resulted from progressively freeing commercial banks to fill their role in contemporary society.

I

It is a curious and interesting fact that in an economic world dominated by the ideal of *laissez faire,* Americans chose first to regulate financial institutions. As early as 1791, with the formation of the first Bank of the United States, the federal government intervened to secure an allocation of financial resources different from what the private sector would have ordered. This intervention so annoyed the owners of state-chartered commercial banks that 20 years later they secured the political end of the first Bank of the United States. History in a sense repeated itself when the second Bank of the United States, established in 1816, failed of recharter largely because of the unremitting opposition of private banking interests. Indeed, for 30 years after Andrew Jackson's veto of the bill to recharter an effective central bank, Americans consistently refused all attempts to link the federal government to financial markets.

In 1863, after more than a year of heated and often noisy debate, Congress passed the Currency Act of 1863, which was shortly recast in the form of the National Bank Act of 1864, still one of the basic banking laws of the land. This legislation permitted a group of bank organizers to obtain a national charter and so brought under federal supervision a major category of business firms.[1] To be sure, this intervention by the national government was prompted in large part by the requirements of financing the Civil War, for it was anticipated that the new national-bank currency, secured by the deposit of government bonds, would stimulate the demand for Treasury issues. Nevertheless, the country reaped the benefit of a uniform currency as well as the continuing advantages of bank supervision with standards far higher than those of most states.

It was clearly the intent of Congress to do away with state-chartered banks when legislation was passed in 1865 placing a prohibitive tax on the note issue of the state institutions. But a few state banks, having found that a circulation was no longer necessary, held on for a transitional period of ten years or so. From the mid-1870s on, state-bank charters became increasingly numerous, and there began a charter race between federal and state authorities that continued for almost half a century. By 1920

[1]With the exception of another category of financial institutions, savings and loan associations, Congress has for more than a century consistently avoided granting charters to strictly private firms.

there were approximately 30,000 banks in this country, some 22,000 with state charters and 8,000 with national charters.

In a sense, the national banking system did all that it was engineered to do. Yet as the 19th century drew to a close, it became progressively evident that the monetary system was seriously defective. The most pressing difficulties occurred when, in times of recurring monetary panic, banks suspended cash payments and the currency supply all but disappeared. Despite a faulty analysis that attributed much of the difficulty to an "inelastic" currency, policymakers at last muddled through to a partial remedy. What was needed, they concluded, was a central institution that could *create* reserves, injecting liquidity at appropriate times. With the passage of the Federal Reserve Act in 1913, Americans reluctantly accepted the idea of a central bank, comforting themselves with the thought that the new institution was not *really* a central bank but 12 regional banks. The framers of the Federal Reserve Act did not intend that the new central bank should execute a monetary policy aimed at stabilizing the economy; in fact, the Federal Reserve did not seriously undertake such a responsibility for almost four decades after its founding. Nevertheless, the public was reassured by the establishment of an institution that hopefully would prevent money panics and so lessen the acute distress of the ensuing depressions.

The newly organized Federal Reserve Board came almost immediately into conflict with the Comptroller of the Currency, who, along with the Secretary of the Treasury, was *ex officio* a member of that Board. After enjoying for half a century a unique position as supervisor of nationally chartered banks, it would have been astonishing indeed if the Comptroller of the Currency had not resisted attempts to dilute his authority. Nor was John Skelton Williams, the Comptroller during the early years of the Federal Reserve, a man inclined to avoid controversy. The upshot of this early skirmishing over questions ranging from the design of examination forms to the geographic organization of the Comptroller's Office was a series of bills aimed at abolishing or subordinating to Federal Reserve authority the Office of the Comptroller of the Currency. But a 1917 amendment to the Federal Reserve Act gave Federal Reserve Banks authority to supervise state-chartered member banks, providing the regional Banks a certain necessary hegemony. A series of more than usually competent Comptrollers from Henry M. Dawes to John W. Pole, plus the political strength of an old bureaucracy, kept inviolate the Comptroller's supervisory authority over national banks. By 1930 relations between the Board and the Comptroller were less strained, though both agencies were still lodged under the massive roof of the Treasury Building.

I need not dwell on the banking difficulties of the 1920s, which worsened steadily during the catastrophe of 1930-33. Federal Reserve authorities, not comprehending the proper role of the central bank in a period of financial emergency, failed to stop the deflation, with the consequence that bank failures increased at a frightening rate. Between 1921 and 1933 some 14,000 banks suspended, nearly 9,000 going under in the four-year span of 1930-33. More than 90 per cent of these failures were in communities with less than 25,000 inhabitants, and 85 per cent of the suspending banks had total assets of less than $1 million. But by early 1933 the virus of failure had spread to large banks in certain metropolitan areas, and the entire system was in danger of complete disintegration. Only the drastic measures of bank moratoria prevented ultimate breakdown.

The disaster of the Great Depression led to changes in the financial system that have their effects in the present day. These changes included an innovation tried intermittently in state jurisdictions for nearly a century, the insurance of bank deposits. First introduced on a temporary basis in the Banking Act of 1933, insurance of bank deposits was made permanent two years later in the Banking Act of 1935. A new agency, the Federal Deposit Insurance Corporation (whose efficiency is still to be tested), was created to undertake the new function, and by the end of 1935 more than 90 per cent of United States commercial banks were covered.

At last most of the state banks that had not elected Federal Reserve membership were brought under the umbrella of federal supervision. In 1938 the three federal agencies agreed to certain uniform procedures and to a division of labor that remains substantially in effect. The FDIC, with the Comptroller of the Currency as a member of its three-man board, supervises non-member insured state banks. Federal Reserve supervises state member banks, and the Comptroller of the Currency supervises national banks. Although the FDIC and Federal Reserve are technically and legally empowered to examine national banks, it is an unusual occasion when these agencies concern themselves with national bank problems.

While the triumvirate of Federal regulatory agencies in some respects dominates bank supervision in this country, 50 state regulatory authorities have a constantly declining, though not insignificant influence. In part this influence results from the fact that a few states, notably New York and California, have a number of large state-chartered banks supervised by fairly well trained, fairly knowledgeable personnel. In part, however, state regulation is significant because in some jurisdictions it is so highly restrictive, particularly with respect to multioffice banking. And in all the jurisdictions state authorities provide more or less vocal channels through which officers and directors of state-chartered banks exercise political influence out of proportion to the banking resources they control.

Anyone who reflects on the historical evolution of the regulatory agencies must be impressed with the oblique way in which each one took over its functions. Supervision by the Comptroller of the Currency started in order to protect the quality of bank-note issue. The Federal Reserve began its supervisory role because of the storm of protest raised by state member banks over examination by the Comptroller of the Currency. And the FDIC backed into the supervisory function because the agency at first wished to make sure that banks were insurable, concluding finally that continuous supervision would be necessary to keep them that way.

More important as a determinant of attitudes toward bank regulation were the pressures under which legislation was passed. The fundamental banking laws of this country have without exception been forged in an emotional climate of reform or crisis. Aimed at removing past evils, they have rapidly become anachronistic. In particular, provisions for bank supervision have looked backward, calculated not so much to win the future as to defeat the past.

For Americans living in the last half of the 20th century, the frustrating and negativistic supervisory attitudes have been in large part those emerging from the Great

Depression, born and hardened in fear. The Banking Acts of 1933 and 1935 can most charitably be characterized as based on serious misconceptions about the causes of economic malaise. But whatever the thinking of those who framed them, these statutes only served to clutter up the law, increasing its publicly harmful duplication, overlap, and unjustifiable waste. A far more serious defect has been the technical and substantive inadequacy of the law to meet the requirements imposed on the financial community in general, and on commercial banks in particular, to meet the needs of a rapidly changing economy. Since there has been no major overhaul of federal banking laws for more than three decades, the problems of achieving genuinely creative bank supervision have become nearly insuperable, even in those rare instances where the supervisory authorities would will otherwise.

II

The past two generations have witnessed remarkable variations in the functions of commercial banks and in the competitive environment within which they have operated. But until well after the end of World War II one characteristic of banking remained invariant: with exceptions that only proved the rule, bank managements were ultra-conservative — plodding, unimaginative, and dull, with a marked tendency to be hereditary, not unlike their counterparts in the supervisory mechanisms. Innovation in such fields as consumer credit was attempted only by the daring, who, while reaping considerable rewards, were considered foolhardy by their colleagues.

The consequence of collective indisposition to innovate was the growing relative importance of nonbank intermediaries—life insurance companies, savings and loan associations, mutual savings banks, finance companies, non-insured pension funds, and credit unions being the most important. In general, commercial banks increased in relative importance during the inflationary periods of two world wars and their immediate aftermaths. But once the rate of growth of the money supply returned to postwar normals, the nonbank intermediaries, which were at once the *customers* and *competitors* of commercial banks, grew relatively while commercial banks retrogressed. This was the pattern of change at least until the early 1960s.

It was in the 19th and early 20th century tradition of American commercial banking that banks came to be primarily committed to short-term, "self-liquidating" paper. During World War I and through the decade of the 1920s bankers considered themselves almost exclusively lenders to business. By present standards loan-to-deposit ratios were extremely high, and cash assets and other securities were considered necessary evils, buffers against the vagaries of an economic climate that might change with savage swiftness. With the onset of the Great Depression, banks reduced their volume of loans greatly, increasing somewhat their holdings of governments. By 1934 the total amount of investments exceeded the amount of loans, though it was not until 1943 that the income from investments exceeded the income from loans. By that time the value of securities owned was twice that of loans outstanding.

In 1945 it looked as though banks had changed from holders of private debt to holders of public debt. Many observers commented that the banking system had ceased to perform its primary function of furnishing short-term credit to commerce and industry, that banks had in fact become investment trusts specializing in Treasury issues.

Supporters of this view contended that bank loans no longer bore a close relationship to industrial production and that there was a growing tendency for banks to keep funds idle in the form of cash assets. Bankers retorted that safe loans could not be made during the 1930s and that the government, by building its own facilities and lending directly to business during World War II, had continued to depress the demand for loans. In effect, bankers argued, banks financed government, which in turn financed private industry.

During the postwar years there was a rapid growth of loans as banks, striving to increase profitability, shifted out of the Treasury issues that an obliging Federal Reserve, until 1951, stood ready to purchase at or above par. By late 1952 loans exceeded holdings of government securities, though other securities weighted the balance on the investment side. In 1955, for both national banks and state member banks, loans surpassed total investments in dollar volume.[2] Even with the return toward a historically normal distribution of assets, many still thought that the economic functions of banks had been permanently modified, that the commercial banking system's role as a residual lender to government would remain about what it was at that time.

Meantime, changes on the liability side of bank statements were on the whole unexciting. At the time of World War I, time deposits began a slow but steady increase in relative importance, during the 1920s gradually approaching demand deposits in total dollar volume. By 1930 they were practically equal in amount, one series indicating that time deposits actually surpassed demand deposits in

---

[2]For state nonmember banks loans did not surpass investments in dollar volume until the end of 1959.

dollar volume for a few months during 1930. But with deepening depression and declining opportunities for high-yield loans, bank managers made only token efforts to attract and hold time deposits, and agnostic attitudes toward aggressive attraction of time deposits became a part of commercial banking mentality for perhaps a quarter of a century. For one had only to look at the appropriate table published each year in the *Federal Reserve Bulletin* to see that, on an average, banks with a high proportion of time to total deposits had less favorable profit ratios than those with a low proportion of time to total deposits.[3] Furthermore, not until the monetary episode of 1959-60 was there a bout with genuinely tight money in the historical sense of the term. Actually, the decade of the 1950s was marked by increasing sub-par performance of the American economy, and bankers were under no particular compulsion to attract funds in order to increase their lending volume.

One further change on the liability side of commercial bank balance sheets requires comment. Capital accounts have not increased since 1920 in anything like the same proportion as deposits; i.e., the ratio of capital accounts to total deposits has fallen. Indeed, as far back as 1890 the ratio was one-third, at the inception of the Federal Reserve it was one-fifth, and sound banking practice prescribed a ratio of no less than one-sixth in the early 1920s. Yet except for the depression years the ratio fell until it approximated one-twelfth in the late 1950s.

Everything considered, it seemed to most observers of the contemporary scene that the banking community of the

---

[3]See, for example, Operating Ratios by Ratio of Time to Total Deposits and by Size of Bank, *Federal Reserve Bulletin,* April, 1965, p. 618.

mid-1950s, stirred by a few leaders in the business, was showing signs of an awakening competitive instinct as had not been witnessed for a generation, but was still happy to settle back into the traditional mold. But younger managers, many of them recruited from the colleges and universities into organized training programs, were beginning to take over policy-making functions. They began to understand that in an economy committed to economic stabilization old rules of thumb about loan-to-deposit ratios, capital-risk asset ratios, and the like were no longer reliable guides to action. More important, though, was the profit motive, which by the late 1950s drove competitive managers to try new ways of obtaining resources. Their main attack was to secure some relaxation of the rigid price-fixing harness which the Federal Reserve kept on the freedom of the banks to compete for funds in the money markets.

Successive changes in Regulation Q, initiated on January 1, 1957, unquestionably paved the way. Between 1948 and 1956 increases in time deposits of commercial banks were moderate, growing at an average yearly rate of 4½ per cent. But between 1956 and 1963, the annual rate of growth of time deposits was 12 per cent. In the absence of any change but that of a single Federal Reserve regulation, the competitive environment of financial institutions would have been affected. But the banking community, flushed with success and enjoying the euphoria of comfortable new physical surroundings, undertook two innovations that halted and perhaps reversed the postwar retrogression of the system. One of these innovations, the negotiable certificate of deposit, its marketability assurred by the issuing banks, need not detain us; for it was a tried and true instrument, invented more than a hundred years ago and in substantial use in the 1920s.

A second new source of funds, far less important in dollar volume of money raised but tremendously important in its effect on lending limits, was the issue of debt obligations by sophisticated bank managements. In a sense, this move should have occasioned no surprise, for banks, more than any other type of business, have long made a practice of trading on their equities. Nevertheless, from the very earliest days of commercial banking in this country there has been a strong aversion to bank borrowing. It is one thing, apparently, to have depositors for creditors and another to have non-depositors for creditors. However this may be, banks have in recent years made growing use of unsecured promissory notes and capital notes and debentures. At the end of 1965, $364 million of the former and $1,134 million of the latter had been issued by national banks. Clearly, both these instruments were made possible by favorable decisions during my tenure. Shortly after taking office, I ruled that "commercial paper, as such notes are commonly described, is a well recognized, useful, and flexible instrument for the acquisition of available short-term capital," that "these notes may be issued at face amount or at a discount, in negotiable or non-negotiable form, and in any maturity," and that "the proceeds may be used for any normal banking purpose."[4] Unlike capital notes and debentures these securities are not subordinated to the rights of depositors. The amounts that banks may borrow by means of unsecured notes are limited by the borrowing limitations contained in 12 U.S.C. 82. These notes are not and cannot be legally considered deposits, and interest ceilings and reserve requirements are therefore not legally applicable. I further ruled that the proceeds

[4] *101st Annual Report,* Comptroller of the Currency, 1963, p. 22.

of capital notes and capital debentures, which are subordinate in right of payment to all deposit liabilities of the issuing bank, could be included as part of the aggregate amount of unimpaired capital and surplus of a bank for the purpose of determining the bank's lending limits.

Thus, though the dollar amount of funds raised in this manner has been small in comparison with total liabilities of commercial banks, borrowing to augment capital has been the most important single variable among several easing lending limits of commercial banks. The inclusion of borrowed money in the capital accounts substantially raised these limits and so made it possible for institutions to accommodate favored customers without sharing their business with participating banks.

When I left office, the staff was inclined to limit indebtedness in the capital accounts to 25 to 30 per cent of the total, though a few large banks then exceeded this percentage. Many commercial bankers were frank to say, however, that they foresaw a time when half the capital accounts would be borrowed; they were equally frank to say that they would do everything they could do to push toward such a limitation.

This hasty review of recent change in the competitive position of commercial banks is only suggestive of the number and complexity of the variables at work. Clearly such major economic forces as prolonged depression, war-induced inflation, a period of rapid growth, or a period of sluggish, sub-par performance can be overpowering for years on end, largely determining the rate of growth of financial institutions and the relative progress of the several intermediaries. Yet rules and regulations of monetary and supervisory authorities have, in the jargon of economics, a marginal effect that on occasion makes the influence of the regulators dominant. So, as we have just observed, small changes in permissible rates payable under Federal Reserve's Regulation Q reversed the decade-long advantage that Savings and Loan Associations had maintained over commercial banks in the competition for savings. And a common-sense ruling of the Comptroller that, like any other corporation, banks should have access to debt as well as equity capital did much to help banks weather the monetary stringency that began in December of 1965.

III

Some years ago, in a journal relatively unfamiliar, there appeared an article entitled "Saxon Versus the Status Quo."[5] To most observers, I suppose, rulings early in my tenure *did* pose a threat to established regulatory procedures. But it was my conviction that we were *preserving* the *status quo* in the sense that we were trying to maintain a centuries-long tradition of competition in business affairs. Only a month previously, in an address titled "The Promise of Free Enterprise," I had remarked:

> Decades of excessive controls have created the image of banking as a closed industry—an industry in which reliance upon governmental protection, and constricted scope for initiative, have become ingrained. This image can be changed only by allowing the burgeoning forces of private enterprise to enter this industry with greater freedom.

This was the guiding principle of my years of public service, that we should allow markets, the price mechanism if you will, to allocate resources in finance as in much of the rest of American business. Having spent a considerable part of my career as a public servant in the Treasury I was as aware as anyone of the requirement that banks be sub-

[5] *Bank Stock Quarterly* (June, 1963), p. 11.

ject to consistent, intelligently ordered supervision. But effective supervisory procedures are certainly not inconsistent with permitting new investment in banking, whether in the form of newly chartered institutions or of increases in size of existing ones.

In this brief compass I can only indicate the direction and scope of our major policy concerns:

(1) *New charters.* The 25-year span 1936-60 was a period of drastic reduction in the rate of formation of new banks. In this period only 335 national banks were chartered, national charters accounting for less than one-fifth of the nearly 2000 banks organized in these years. Beginning in 1962, the Office of the Comptroller encouraged applications for new charters; in 1961 only 97 applications were received, but in 1962 the number rose to 176 and went up to 490 in 1963 and 468 in 1964. In the 4-year period 1962-65 the Office granted 513 new charters, while state authorities, probably stimulated to greater liberality by our actions, granted 502. Banking resources were increased in trade areas where they had been deficient; yet we at all times showed due concern to prevent overinvestment in banking, announcing from time to time that applications from particular areas would be rejected once a certain level of investment was reached. Actually, the rate of charter rejections for 1965 was 70 per cent.

(2) *Approval of branches.* In 1900, banks with branches accounted for only two per cent of resources of American commercial banks. But in ensuing decades the economic forces compelling the growth of branch banking were inexorable; and by 1935, branch banks controlled more than one-half the resources of commercial banks. The trend toward branches continued, and it was the policy of the Office during my tenure to encourage the healthy growth

of branch-bank systems. From the end of 1960 to the end of 1965, the number of national banks maintaining branches rose from 905 to 1,331, an increase of 48 per cent; in this same period the number of branches operated by national banks rose 64 per cent. (Branches of state banks rose in this interim by 37 per cent.) Despite the ill-advised maintenance of "unit" banking in some states, branch banks controlled approximately two-thirds of the banking resources of the country by the end of 1965.

(3) *Action on mergers.* In our continuing efforts to assure a new and vital competition among commercial banks and between commercial banks and nonbank intermediaries, the Office held open the option of merger where in our judgment banking resources would be more effectively allocated and there were no serious competitive disadvantages. Decisions in the *Philadelphia* and *Lexington* cases subjected commercial banks to more stringent antitrust regulation than applies to firms in unregulated industry, and the Bank Merger Act of 1966, while clarifying the standards by which merger decisions shall be made by the banking agencies, still permits the Department of Justice to postpone mergers through court action.

In a word, it was the policy of the Office during my tenure to assure the economic entry of resources into commercial banking by means that appeared appropriate in each particular case. But principles and policies can only be effected through decisions, interpretations and actions. Of the thousands of specific determinations made during a tenure of five years, some were bound to cause controversy.

My successors in the Office of the Comptroller, as well as succeeding incumbents in other agency offices, would be greatly helped by statutory changes that would codify and clarify present intricate and overlapping relationships.

Ideally, I suppose, commercial banking should be subject to a single federal regulatory authority, but the theoretical and practical advantages of such an arrangement, while clearly demonstrable, probably could not be achieved without long and divisive argument, if, indeed, they could be legislated at all in our present environment. Moreover, there is much to be gained by less drastic legislation along the lines of the Financial Institutions Act of 1957, which had sufficient merit to secure passage by the Senate. If that temperate and reasonable act, calculated to bring permissive bank practices and the supervision of banking into the 20th century, had become law, nearly all the actions and decisions of my tenure as Comptroller would have seemed routine.

When law fails to keep pace with social change, public administrators and judges must make ever broader interpretations under the constraints of antiquated and ambiguous statutes and administrative decisions of days long past. The haste with which I moved during the first three years of my tenure appeared precipitate to many observers. But change is likely to seem sudden and uncomfortable when it is consequent upon the release of forces artifically held in check for years or even decades.

I referred in my final *Annual Report* to the rise of a new enthusiasm in commercial banking, an *esprit* that will carry the industry forward to new peaks of service to the community. The momentum of the industry should benefit even nonbank institutions with which they compete, provided that competition is in the market place and not among lobbyists and bureaucrats who seek to destroy competition through selfish and damaging legislation. The social advantages of a vital commercial banking system, unfettered by statutes passed in some instances a century ago, should be apparent to Congress and the people, and there is reason to hope that banking law will soon be brought up to date.

Meantime, we can only hope that the regulatory authorities will not continue to dance backwards together within the trammels of dogma handed down in a long-past day and time, but on the contrary, will seek creative, forward-looking, supervisory and regulatory policies. In due course, it is imperative that the Congress legislate consolidation of all commercial banks' supervision and regulation into one single federal authority. Fifty-seven separate supervisory and regulatory agencies will otherwise strangle and suffocate the commercial banking industry.

Lecture Three

by Pierre-Paul Schweitzer

It gives me much pleasure to be associated with the inaugural series of M. L. Seidman Memorial Lectures sponsored by your enlightened University. I am sure that this new venture will soon be established as a notable event not only in the life of this community but also farther afield. My distinguished predecessors in the series have dealt with important aspects of public financial policy in its domestic context. I wish to discuss the related field of international finance with especial reference to the role of the International Monetary Fund.

* * *

It is now 20 years since the Fund began its financial operations with member countries. This is moreover a time when the international monetary system is the subject of much comment in the press and elsewhere, not all of it of a favorable or flattering kind. Indeed, one might well be excused for wondering what kind of system this is that seems in constant need of repair and reconstruction, and what kind of monetary managers we are who seem so dilatory in putting things right. This impression is understandable. In my view it is also quite false. I say this not in any guise of counsel for the defense, still less as apologist for the status quo, but because I believe that these immediate concerns must properly be seen in a wider and longer perspective.

One reason why discussion of international monetary questions often seems rather bewildering, even to many specialists, is simply that the view is too close and so lacks focus. The international monetary system, and the role of the Fund in it, have been evolving rapidly in recent years. This is a field where the status quo has a habit of never standing still. Sometimes our existing system is portrayed as fusty and antiquated in contrast to a beckoning prospect of entirely different character, which could materialize if only the powers that be would reach agreement amongst themselves. Such conceptions bear little relationship to the real world. Certainly important decisions must be taken, and much care and thought is being given to them. But they will be part of a continuing evolution, which over the years has wrought profound changes in the system. These changes are not always embodied in legal documents or even in informal agreements, but may be the result of new developments in the world's business and banking community, which is in a sense the very basis of the system.

A historical perspective

In an effort to achieve some perspective, I would suggest that the impression, so easily gained from public discussion, that our modern monetary arrangements are under unprecedented critical fire does not withstand the most cursory historical analysis. For a very long time there has been fierce debate about the rules under which international monetary transactions should take place. Between the two world wars the argument swayed to and fro on what was generally referred to as "The Gold Problem." First, fears were expressed about a threatening gold shortage and about a corresponding need for gold economy. Then, after the system broke under strain and a broad depreciation in exchange rates came about, there was even some apprehension voiced about the danger of a golden avalanche. Here was one of those 180 degree turns that have sometimes made laymen throw up their hands at the apparent capriciousness of international monetary problems. Still earlier, the end of the nineteenth century had seen the climax of the great debates, even more intensive in the United States than in Europe, over the nature of the metallic monetary standard, when gold won a decisive victory over silver. In the first half of the nineteenth century, there had been the debates both on the appropriate scope for paper money and on the extent of the banking process. These were conducted essentially in a domestic context, but they provide some interesting parallels with modern discussions on the degree to which those concepts can or should be applied internationally.

Nor should one suppose that the issues involved in the monetary debates of earlier generations were any less substantive or keenly felt than those in our own times. Money, in its national and global role no less than on a more personal level, has always exercised the emotions as well as the intellect. This also is understandable, since monetary technicalities often go to the heart of much wider, political issues on which political decisions have to be made. Yet the dramatization and occasional polarization of monetary issues have not always been conducive to the quickest understanding of those issues, or to attainment of the optimum solution.

What *is* a distinctive feature of the present, most recent installment in these long historical debates is that the accepted area of economic policy has widened. And the implications of this are so pervasive that our institutional arrangements, both domestically and internationally, have still to be fully adapted to the pursuit by national governments of more positive and extensive economic policy goals. To be sure, concern with the monetary standard has long been related to wider ends—conditions of trade, opportunities for employment, the level of prices, and the like. But the older assumption was that adoption of the appropriate system of stable money was itself an adequate contribution by public policy toward these goals. Thus, before 1914, financial stability, conceived rather narrowly in terms of effective exchange stability rather than price stability, was regarded, if not as an end in itself, as a virtually sufficient means to the wider economic ends then seen as desirable.

In modern times, however, governments have increasingly accepted responsibility for the general performance of their economies in terms of avoiding needless unemployment and reaching the highest sustainable rate of growth, while striving still to maintain both exchange and price stability. The pursuit of these multiple aims is clearly much more demanding than the more restricted concern with exchange stability was in earlier days; and in this sense modern monetary management is altogether more ambitious than any attempted before. In the domestic context alone, the aims of full employment and maximum economic growth can, as we all know, put severe strains on price stability; and since virtually all our modern economies are in some degree open economies, these strains are soon transmitted to the balance of payments with the rest of the world. The need to reconcile domestic objectives with a due balance in international payments is, to be sure, a constraint on policy, rather than a policy aim in itself. Beyond a point, balance is no longer a matter of choice: the only question is how it is brought about. Unless there exists an effective and orderly process of adjustment, the risk is that external balance may come about through the sacrifice of other important objectives. In particular, relief from payments strains may be sought through the creation of artificial barriers to international trade; through restrictions on foreign investment; through retrenchment in aid disbursed to poorer countries; or through disruptive changes in exchange rates. Defensive measures of this kind taken by countries under financial pressure are generally detrimental to the international community and may quickly infect it by provoking retaliation. History is not short of examples in which over-rapid adjustment of payments *balances* has had deleterious effects. Clearly, after World War II, it was of great benefit to Western Europe that the adjustment in its payments deficit with the United States could be spread over a comfortable period. But in recent years adjustments to payments imbalances, both deficits and surpluses, have tended to be too slow rather than too fast.

It is in the broad aim of helping countries to meet their domestic economic objectives without unnecessary damage to themselves and their neighbors in their international transactions that the genesis of the International Monetary Fund is to be found. The Fund belongs to the family of international institutions established right after World War II. The concern of its founders was to avoid the kind of economic conflicts that had plagued the interwar years, in which the financial discipline and economic internationalism of the gold standard could neither prevent nor survive the calamity of the world depression, and in which the slow and painful recovery from that depression was too often on the basis of protectionist and nationalist policies—or beggar-my-neighbor policies, as they were aptly called. The Fund began its life with some 30 member countries; by the late 1950s membership was around the 60 mark; and the next few years saw its own population explosion, so that its present membership numbers 106. It includes almost all countries outside Russia and Eastern Europe. The Fund is the one world-wide body that is charged with the general responsibility for the good functioning of the international monetary system.

Let me comment now on some aspects of that system, before turning to the specific functions of the Fund and its role in recent international financial developments.

The nature of the system

The international monetary system, in its widest sense, includes all the business and financial organizations and the institutional facilities which make possible the transfer of funds across national borders. International payments are made for much the same range of transactions as take place within national economies—for movements of goods, in foreign trade; for provision of services, in what the balance of payments statisticians refer to with some feeling as "invisible items"; for investment outlays, whether by business firms in overseas plants or acquisition of subsidiaries, which we call direct investment, or for purchase of portfolio securities; and finally, for settlement of various kinds of past debts. Aside from a relatively small category of payments made directly between governments or central banks, the great bulk of these payments is handled by and through commercial banks and other private institutions. These institutions clear and settle the resulting mass of claims and counter claims in different currencies through the mechanism of the foreign exchange market which they form for this purpose.

What happens from then on determines, and is determined by, the particular nature of the payments system. Under the old gold standard, the major commercial countries adhering to it fixed the value of their currency in terms of gold, allowed holders of the currency to convert it into gold at this fixed value, and further allowed gold to be imported and exported freely, or at least without undue hindrance. The important by-product of these arrangements was that, since each individual currency had a fixed value in terms of gold, it also had an almost fixed exchange value in terms of the other currencies in the system, in the way that two quantities that are equivalent to a third will also be equivalent to each other. In the actual workings of the exchange market, this stabilization of currency values took place basically through private arbitrage in gold between different centers, and often through anticipation of such arbitrage. Adjustment to gold losses under this system, though by no means so automatic as is sometimes imagined, often proceeded through rather harsh disruptions in the domestic economy, of a kind that would not be compatible with modern domestic goals in the field of employment and growth.

After this system broke down in the early 1930s, fixed links between the major currencies were for a time abandoned altogether, and exchange rates were determined from day to day by the pull of all the various influences in the exchange markets, not infrequently dominated by destabilizing bouts of intense speculative activity. Yet these were still not entirely free exchange markets since the forces at work also included new official stabilization funds. These funds intervened in the market to prevent, or at least moderate, unwanted movements in exchange rates. This quickly led to the danger of mutual conflict between the aims of different funds; and the experience is worth recalling. The increased responsibilities of economic management which governments were accepting made them still less willing to leave the movement of their exchange rates entirely outside their control; yet neither could they each retain such control by independent action, since every exchange transaction affects the exchange value of not one currency but two. Such considerations led already in the second half of the 1930s to limited moves toward exchange stabilization and the beginnings of certain ground rules for exchange intervention.

This was the background for the new exchange regime which was written into the Fund's Articles of Agreement, and which has become known as the par value system. Promotion of exchange stability is laid down as one of the basic purposes of the International Monetary Fund. Members agree to establish with the Fund a par value for their currency, expressed in terms of gold or of the U.S. dollar of the weight and fineness in effect on July 1, 1944. Recognizing that any change in their par value is a matter of common concern, members undertake to refrain from such action except to correct a fundamental disequilibrium in their payments; and even then they may act only after consultation with the Fund and, save in certain circumstances, only with its concurrence. This regime was designed to provide the basic advantages of exchange stability by establishing a fixed frame of reference for international payments without the extreme rigidity of the completely fixed exchange values of the gold standard. It sought, that is, to avoid both the arbitrary fluctuations and the ultimately brittle inflexibility of which the world had had such painful experience in the interwar years. Judged in this light, and by the tremendous expansion of world production and trade that has accompanied it, the present system deserves better marks than many theorists seem inclined to concede it.

An essential element in the par value system is that members of the Fund undertake to maintain the spot rate for their currency within a limited margin—no more than one per cent—on either side of parity. They do so through intervention by their official funds in the exchange markets. Such intervention is conducted in the main against the U.S. dollar and the normal processes of arbitrage insure that stability against the dollar is reflected in stability against other currencies too. The prominent exception to this practice occurs in the case of the United States, which takes advantage of the provision in the Fund Articles stating that a member whose monetary authorities, for the settlement of international transactions, freely buy and sell gold within prescribed limits, shall be deemed to be fulfilling its undertaking in respect to exchange stability. The undertaking by the U.S. Treasury in this regard underpins the par value of the U.S. dollar and has contributed to its widespread use by other countries as an intervention and reserve currency. For the gold window of the U.S. Treasury affords foreign official holders of dollars an indirect link between gold and their own currency and so gives the dollar an extra dimension as an international currency.

The functions of the Fund

But the par value system is not to be viewed in isolation. It forms an integral part of the IMF system, which must be seen as a whole. Promotion of general exchange stability is supported by the availability of Fund credits to supplement the reserves of member countries in payments deficit. The purpose of these credits is to afford members time to make orderly adjustments, "without resorting to measures destructive of national or international prosperity." The Fund Articles of Agreement refer specifically to the promotion and maintenance of high levels of employment and real income and to the development of productive resources of all members. They also embody a code of good conduct administered by the Fund and based on the avoidance of payments restrictions for current international transactions and on the maintenance of a multilateral system of payments. These triple functions of the Fund in its exchange rate role, its regulatory role, and its lending role, are in a sense bound together by its consultative function. The Fund has gradually built up close and continuous working contact with its member countries, and attaches great importance to this side of its work. For the influence of the Fund with its members, and the help it can offer them, depend to an important degree on its own understanding of their particular circumstances, and on mutual trust of a kind that can be fostered only by a long and continuous working contact.

Has this IMF system worked in practice? The broad answer is undeniably: Yes. Since the major currency realignment of 1949, which should itself be regarded as a part of postwar reconstruction, exchange rates of the leading industrial countries have been broadly stable. At the same time the system has been flexible enough to encompass some necessary individual adjustments. Competitive currency depreciation, the great bane of the financial world in the 1930s, has been entirely absent. Nor, for the most part, has the world suffered extensively from what may be seen as an opposite danger, of overvalued currencies maintained at fixed exchange rates through restrictions on trade and payments, harming both the country imposing them and the international community. During the 1950s, fairly steady progress was made in freeing international transactions from such restrictions. In 1961, the leading European countries undertook to perform their formal Fund obligations to maintain convertibility of their currencies and avoid payments restrictions.

These formal commitments to the Fund relate only to payments for current transactions. No such commitments exist for capital movements. But during the general postwar liberalization of payments this distinction was found to be not always practicable or desirable, so that by about 1960 capital was again moving freely across national frontiers, for short-term financial arbitrage as well as for longer-term investment. In recent years, however, there has been a distinct change in policy in this sphere. Controls on the movement of funds and on international lending have tended to creep back; and even the United States has introduced a measure of selective restraint on capital transfers abroad. For the most part, such tendencies are to be regretted. This is not to say that the issues involved are always clear cut. Short-term defensive considerations may pull against longer-term objectives. And international capital movements can take many forms. These forms include the generally unpopular and disturbing category of flight money, reacting to sometimes irrational fears about currency values or political influences. It was perhaps chiefly these kinds of capital flows that the founders of the Fund had in mind when they gave member countries freedom to control capital movements.

On the other hand short-term funds can also move in very large quantities in response to more normal economic influences, such as differences in international interest rates and business conditions. There is nowadays an undoubted tendency toward speedy interaction among national money markets, a tendency which has been strong enough to overpower a wide array of restrictions and special institutional arrangements designed to insulate these markets. A vigorously expanding market in dollar deposits placed and taken among banks outside the United States—the Euro-dollar market—has become an important repository for liquid funds of commercial banks and other institutions. In the past few years, moreover, the rapid extension of overseas branches by U.S. banks and consequent transfers of funds between these branches and their head offices have increased the sensitivity of the rest of the world to developments in the U.S. money market. In this context the experience of 1966 recalled certain aspects of the international money market before 1914, when a tightening of credit in the center of the system—then London—quickly brought a shift of funds from the periphery.

There may indeed be certain instances where national monetary authorities feel unduly exposed to the movement of volatile international funds. At the same time considerable progress has been made in guiding or containing these money flows through official action on interest rates and in the forward exchange markets. For the rest, there seems widespread agreement that, rather than attempting to forestall or restrict short-term movements through physical controls, it is often both preferable and more practicable to absorb any disturbing influences through offsetting transfers of official funds. This may well be a continuing function for short-term credits granted between central banks. These credits, or swap arrangements, have been expanded in a major way in this decade, in the first instance to deal with speculative movements. But they are specifically intended for very short-term use and, in some cases, obligations have in effect been funded through drawings on the International Monetary Fund.

The resources of the Fund are designed in all cases for temporary rather than long-term use by its members, but the time scale here is measured in years rather than months. Drawings are intended to tide countries over a reasonable period in which a deficit in their balance of payments is corrected either by self-adjusting influences, which may sometimes be present in the case of seasonal or cyclical deficits or else in response to the necessary policies by the member concerned without too abrupt an adjustment in its domestic economy. Repayments of drawings from the Fund take place both automatically, under a formula which takes into account increases in the borrowing country's own reserves, and in any case within three to five years.

The basic resources of the Fund are subscribed by its members according to their particular quotas. One quarter of a member's quota is normally subscribed to the Fund in gold; the remainder is paid in its own currency. Aggregate quotas amount at present to $21 billion. This is an exaggerated measure of the amounts the Fund can disburse in accordance with its accepted principles of operation, because the currencies of economically weak countries cannot sensibly be used. Nevertheless, the Fund's available resources in gold and usable currencies are substantial. Moreover, as I shall explain later, the Fund can and does supplement its basic resources by borrowing. In its operations the Fund may be likened to a currency pool. When members draw on the Fund, they purchase foreign exchange against further in-payments of their own currency. The member whose currency is purchased in this way thereby increases its own future drawing rights; it may also reduce its net indebtedness to the Fund if it had itself drawn earlier, or if Fund holdings of its currency otherwise exceeded 75 per cent of its quota.

Drawings on the Fund for balance of payments support have grown increasingly important in recent years as a supplement to countries' centrally held reserves. And, as I shall mention later, they have also had the important by-product of adding to world reserves as a whole.

Since the Fund began operations in March 1947, the equivalent of over $13 billion of currencies has been drawn. Between 1947 and 1956, the annual average was $191 million; between 1957 and 1963, it rose to the equivalent of $739 million; and from 1964 through 1966, when drawings were consistently very large, it amounted to the equivalent of over $1,944 million. There has clearly been a rising total demand for the use of Fund resources. More than 65 countries have drawn on the Fund. For many developing countries the Fund has become an important source of balance of payments financing; but drawings have also been an important source of financing for industrial countries such as the United Kingdom, the

United States, France, Canada, Japan, Italy, and the Netherlands. Of the leading industrial members, only Sweden and the Federal Republic of Germany have had no recourse to Fund assistance.

In the course of its extensive financial operations, the Fund has developed, on the basis of its Articles, certain principles designed to enhance the revolving character of its resources and at the same time provide member countries with a reasonable degree of assurance of the facilities they may expect. Access to the Fund's resources is available most freely to those members whose net outstanding drawings from the Fund, other than under a special facility known as compensatory financing, are less than their initial gold in-payments. More precisely, this very liberal treatment is accorded in the measure that the Fund's holding of the member's currency, after adjustment for compensatory financing, is less than 100 per cent of quota. In these "gold tranche" positions, which may include "super-gold tranche" positions arising basically from net use of the currency in drawings by other members, access to Fund resources is available virtually automatically to any member in good standing that can represent a balance of payments need. Beyond this, there are four credit tranches, each equivalent to 25 per cent of quota; and drawings through the range require a rising degree of justification, although in the first credit tranche the Fund policy is still a liberal one. The normal though not invariable limit on drawings—and again I exclude compensatory financing —is reached when a member's outstanding indebtedness becomes equivalent to 125 per cent of its quota; or, to put it another way, when the Fund's holding of its currency rises to 200 per cent of quota.

Within this general framework, the Fund has developed its lending policies in a number of ways. The decision fifteen years ago to permit special treatment of drawings within the basic and super-gold tranches is itself one example. Another is the creation and development of stand-by arrangements—or lines of credit—for members that seek a firm advance assurance of Fund assistance and are willing equally for the Fund to make its own advance appraisal. Most countries drawing on the Fund now do so under stand-bys, which are an especially useful form of wedding the Fund's lending function to its consultative function. In recent years, as I have already noted, the Fund has also offered special compensatory financing facilities to those countries, particularly primary producing countries, which encounter difficulties owing to a temporary short-fall in export receipts for causes generally beyond their control, such as declines in world commodity prices. Recourse to this facility, while increasing Fund holdings of the drawing member's currency, does not have the usual effect of thereby invoking closer scrutiny of future drawings.

The Fund, then, has acquired a special role in the international monetary system by virtue of the sizable resources at its disposal, the revolving nature of its operations and the particular purpose of its operations. It is worth noting too that the Fund's readiness to extend financial assistance to a member country is frequently taken by other potential lenders as evidence that that country is adopting sound economic policies which justify their making further funds available. As I indicated earlier, the Fund is more than a source of balance of payments financing. In an important sense, it is the center of a network of international monetary cooperation which has become as distinguishing a feature of the postwar world as the lack of it was one of the tragedies of the interwar period. The Executive Board, which sits in Washington, has 20 Executive Directors appointed or elected by 106 member countries. The Board deals with a great variety of international monetary problems of both a general and a very specific kind. The Fund staff, which now numbers nearly 900, comprises economists, lawyers and other technically competent people drawn from 62 countries. Through frequent and thorough consultations with member countries the Fund keeps in close touch with economic developments and policies throughout the world. It also provides a variety of services to member countries in the general field of training and technical assistance, which is an increasingly important part of its work.

I noted earlier that over the last few years the operational aspect of the Fund has had an increasingly important by-product: the creation of international reserves. This development has stemmed from the special access to Fund resources available to members with gold tranche positions or their equivalent. These drawing rights are for all practical purposes automatically available and can therefore be counted as effective international reserves. To the extent that these reserve positions in the Fund reflect no more than member countries' own in-payments of gold in relation to their quotas, they represent a change in the form of world reserves, not an addition to the total. But, beyond this, reserve positions in the Fund are established and increased through the use of members' currencies in drawings. As a country establishes a net creditor position in the Fund in this way, it receives a corresponding and unconditional right to draw upon the Fund itself to meet a balance of payments need. When, in the typical case, these transactions also involve a net increase in drawings outstanding in the credit tranches, the result is a creation of new reserves to this extent, although there may be other important side effects. Additional reserves have further been created on the limited occasions when the Fund has used part of its gold for gold investment or general deposits in its gold account.

In the early years of the Fund, virtually the only currency used in drawings was the United States dollar; and the dollar continued to account for the greater part of each year's drawing until 1961. Since then, an increasing number of currencies has been used, not only those of other industrial countries but also, recently, those of some developing countries. In this context I may cite Malaysian dollars, Mexican pesos, Brazilian new cruzeiros, and Venezuelan bolivares. The broad aim has been to encourage more countries in a sound payments and reserve position to hold an appropriate proportion of their reserves through the Fund, while still avoiding recourse to countries currently facing payments difficulties and perhaps likely to request a drawing themselves. In all, 18 currencies have been used in Fund drawings and I have no doubt that more will be added in due course. This extension reflects both the wider spread of financial strength around the world and an increasing awareness among surplus countries that reserve positions in the Fund constitute an appropriate medium for their external reserves. Of course, the Fund can use only the currencies of members in a satisfactory payments and reserve position. It would serve no point to make the currency of a weak country available to another weak country.

Reserve positions are also established when members lend their currencies to the Fund to supplement the basic resources which it has derived from quota payments. This has been done mainly through the General Arrangements to Borrow, under which as a group ten industrial countries stand ready to lend their currencies to the Fund for certain drawings by participants in the group, specifically to "forestall or cope with an impairment of the international monetary system." Resources available under the G.A.B. amount to the equivalent of $6 billion; and the equivalent of $930 million was borrowed by the Fund in this way when the United Kingdom made drawings some two years ago. In addition, on the occasion of a drawing by the United States, the Fund recently borrowed $250 million in Italian lire, in a bilateral transaction under the Fund's general borrowing power.

Developments in world reserves

As a result of the large rise in transactions financed through the Fund, as well as of increases in quotas, total reserve positions in the Fund have expanded very sharply in recent years, from $2.6 billion at the end of 1958 to $6.3 billion at the end of 1966. World reserves at the end of last year amounted in all to some $71 billion, of which Fund reserve positions represented about 9 per cent. Countries' official holdings of foreign exchange, at nearly $24 billion, made up over 33 per cent; and their monetary gold holdings, at about $41 billion, constituted more than 57 per cent. In terms of the total stock of existing reserve assets, the order of importance is therefore gold, foreign exchange, and reserve positions in the Fund. But a striking feature of reserve developments since about the end of 1964 is that, measured by the accretion to this stock, the order of importance is reversed. That is to say, the traditional components of official reserves have become comparatively less significant as generators of additional liquidity.

The absorption of gold into world monetary stocks, which between 1948 and 1964 had been increasing by an average of around 1½ per cent a year, has since virtually ceased: total official holdings, including those of international institutions, were little higher at the end of 1966 than they had been two years earlier. A number of influences have been at work, including a slackening in the growth of gold production, an increase in the use of gold for jewelry as well as for certain industrial purposes, and a continued substantial diversion into idle or speculative hoards.

Movements in countries' foreign exchange holdings have also taken a new turn in the past two years or so. Between the end of 1948 and the end of 1964, official holdings rose from a little more than $13 billion to something over $23 billion. Virtually the whole of this increase was in the form of U.S. dollars. Official reserves held in sterling, which as recently as 1951 were almost twice as large as official dollar holdings, have changed little on balance since the end of World War II, so that by 1964 the dollar component in world reserves was in turn twice as large as the sterling component. Additions to reserves in the form of foreign exchange, or holdings of reserve currencies, are governed basically by two influences. The first is the extent of any net outflow of these currencies from the reserve center countries, responding chiefly to their balance of payments deficits; and the second is the degree to which other countries then choose to retain these currencies in their reserves. In 1965, total official holdings of foreign exchange fell by almost $1 billion, although this was more than offset by a renewed rise in 1966. In both years, however, a major feature was an increase in holdings of foreign exchange by the two main reserve centers themselves, the United States and the United Kingdom, for the most part in the currency of the other. Indeed foreign exchange holdings of third countries at the end of 1966, in total a little over $21 billion, were slightly less than they had been three years earlier.

Among the special influences swelling these cross-holdings of foreign exchange by the reserve centers, and also adding temporarily to foreign exchange holdings of other countries, was the activation of central banking swap facilities, mainly in connection with support operations for sterling. In addition, the U.K. drawings on the Fund in 1964 and 1965 substantially augmented the increase in reserve positions in the Fund during this period. It follows that an unusually large portion of recent reserve growth reflects temporary influences which, other things being equal, will be reversed as repayments are made. And the United Kingdom has now repaid the whole of its short-term credits from central banks and expects to complete repayment of the first $1 billion of its Fund drawings this year.

Assessment of the appropriate level of world reserves, and of the appropriate rate of reserve growth, is still an undeniably difficult task. The indications of a global insufficiency of reserves must essentially be sought in the condition of the world economy and in the economic preoccupations of the leading trading countries. If many are trying to gain reserves and few are willing to lose them, an increase in world liquidity will be necessary to avert the general danger that policies oriented toward gaining or conserving reserves will take priority over other economic objectives. These include the pursuit of a rate of growth compatible with internal financial stability; avoidance of restrictions on international trade and investment; and not least, an adequate flow of aid to poorer countries. At the same time, it is clearly undesirable that the level and growth of international reserves should be of an order that threatens general price stability by encouraging countries to allow their payments deficits to become too large or to run uncorrected.

The reserve developments and related considerations which I have just outlined constitute the background to the current international discussions on whether the supply of reserves from traditional sources should be deliberately supplemented; and by what means this might be done. These discussions have now extended over a period of about three years. Until recently they were conducted, in parallel, in the Fund Executive Board and among the Deputies of the Finance Ministers and Central Bank Governors of the ten industrial countries participating in the General Arrangements to Borrow. Since last fall, however, these two efforts have been concerted in joint meetings of the two bodies, of which three have so far taken place. In this combined forum, all members of the Fund can feel that their interests are fully safeguarded in discussions which are of real importance to all of them, in that their outcome is likely to affect the international monetary system for a long period ahead.

There seems now to be universal agreement that the reserve base of the system should be brought under deliberate control; and agreement on this broad principle can in itself be seen as a major step forward. The discussions have, moreover, done much to clarify the issues and narrow the choices. They have dealt with such questions as the form which any new reserve asset should take, where some favor an automatic drawing right and others a reserve unit; the range of countries to which it should be distributed; the criteria by which decisions on deliberate reserve creation should be guided; and, perhaps most difficult of all, the decision making process itself. On some of these matters agreement seems to have been reached, as in the position that any newly created reserves should be distributed to all members of the Fund in proportion to their Fund quotas or a closely related objective criterion; and that all countries should participate in the process of decision making. Other issues still require more probing and, ultimately, hard negotiation.

Historians may come to say that the world made speedier progress in these two decades toward the management of money internationally than it had done earlier on the road to domestic monetary management. We should not suppose that we have earned any such place in monetary history yet; and no long-run perspective can serve to obscure the urgency of current endeavors to agree on an acceptable mechanism and suitable safeguards. The stakes are high, but I am hopeful that this unfinished work will be brought to a satisfactory conclusion.